THE BOOK OF WITTY ONE-LINERS

COMPILED BY

MANHARDEEP SINGH

ISBN: 978-1-0766-6452-5

1. Knowledge is knowing a tomato is a fruit. Wisdom is not putting a tomato in a fruit salad.

2. The early bird might get the worm, but the second mouse gets the cheese.

3. Children: You spend the first two years of their life teaching them how to walk and talk. The next sixteen? Spent telling them to sit down and shut up.

4. He who smiles in a crisis has found someone to blame.

5. My mother never realized the irony in calling me a son-of-a-bitch.

6. Politicians and diapers have one thing in common. They should both be changed regularly, and for the same reason.

7. I thought I wanted a career, turns out I just wanted paychecks.

8. If I agreed with you, we'd both be wrong.

9. To steal ideas from one person is plagiarism. To steal from many is research.

10. I asked God for a bike, but I know God doesn't work that way. So I stole a bike and asked for forgiveness.

11. Light travels faster than sound. This is why some people appear bright until you hear them speak.

12. We live in society where pizza gets to your house faster than the police.

13. A bus station is where a bus stops. A train station is where a train stops. On my desk, I have a work station.

14. I should have known it wasn't going to work out between my ex-wife and me. After all, I'm a Libra and she's a bitch.

15. How is it one careless match can start a forest fire, but it takes a whole box to start a campfire?

16. I didn't fight my way to the top of the food chain to be a vegetarian.

17. A computer once beat me at chess, but it was no match for me at kick boxing.

18. I saw a woman wearing a sweat shirt with "Guess" on it... so I said "implants?"

19. The shinbone is a device for finding furniture in a dark room.

20. Good girls are bad girls that never get caught.

21. Laugh at your problems, everybody else does.

22. Crowded elevators smell different to midgets.

23. The main reason Santa is so jolly is because he knows where all the bad girls live.

24. Did you know that dolphins are so smart that within a few weeks of captivity, they can train people to stand on the very edge of the pool and throw them fish?

25. God must love stupid people. He made SO many.

26. I didn't say it was your fault. I said I was blaming you.

27. Fighting for peace is like fucking for virginity.

28. Always borrow money from a pessimist. He won't expect it back.

29. Some people say "If you can't beat them, join them". I say "If you can't beat them, beat them", because they will be expecting you to join them, so you will have the element of surprise.

30. Never hit a man with glasses. Hit him with a baseball bat.

31. We have enough gun control. What we need is idiot control.

32. A diplomat is someone who can tell you to go to hell in such a way that you will look forward to the trip.

33. Money can't buy happiness, but it sure makes misery easier to live with.

34. Some cause happiness wherever they go. Others... whenever they go.

35. I discovered I scream the same way whether I'm about to be devoured by a great white shark or if a piece of seaweed touches my foot.

36. War does not determine who is right. It determines who is left.

37. Do not argue with an idiot. He will drag you down to his level and beat you with experience.

38. I want to die peacefully in my sleep, like my grandfather.. Not screaming and yelling like the passengers in his car.

39. The last thing I want to do is hurt you. But it's still on the list.

40. We never really grow up, we only learn how to act in public.

41. Going to church doesn't make you a Christian any more than standing in a garage makes you a car.

42. Evening news is where they begin with 'Good evening', and then proceed to tell you why it isn't.

43. If sex is a pain in the ass, then you're doing it wrong…

44. If you think nobody cares if you're alive, try missing a couple of payments.

45. Better to remain silent and be thought a fool, than to speak and remove all doubt.

46. If God is watching us, the least we can do is be entertaining.

47. If 4 out of 5 people SUFFER from diarrhoea… does that mean that

one enjoys it?

48. Never, under any circumstances, take a sleeping pill and a laxative on the same night.

49. A bank is a place that will lend you money, if you can prove that you don't need it.

50. Why does someone believe you when you say there are four billion stars, but check when you say the paint is wet?

51. Whenever I fill out an application, in the part that says "If an emergency, notify:" I put "DOCTOR". What's my mother going to do?

52. A clear conscience is usually the sign of a bad memory.

53. The voices in my head may not be real, but they have some good ideas!

54. Artificial intelligence is no match for natural stupidity.

55. Crowded elevators smell different to midgets.

56. Behind every successful man is his woman. Behind the fall of a successful man is usually another woman.

57. You do not need a parachute to skydive. You only need a parachute to skydive twice.

58. Never get into fights with ugly people, they have nothing to lose.

59. It's not the fall that kills you; it's the sudden stop at the end.

60. Why do Americans choose from just two people to run for president and 50 for Miss America?

61. My opinions may have changed, but not the fact that I am right.

62. I intend to live forever. So far, so good.

63. My psychiatrist told me I was crazy and I said I want a second opinion. He said okay, you're ugly too.

64. Hospitality: making your guests feel like they're at home, even if you wish they were.

65. I got in a fight one time with a really big guy, and he said, "I'm going to mop the floor with your face." I said, "You'll be sorry." He said, "Oh, yeah? Why?" I said, "Well, you won't be able to get into the corners very well."

66. Worrying works! 90% of the things I worry about never happen.

67. When in doubt, mumble.

68. I always take life with a grain of salt, …plus a slice of lemon, …and a shot of tequila.

69. There's a fine line between cuddling and holding someone down so they can't get away.

70. A little boy asked his father, "Daddy, how much does it cost to get married?" Father replied, "I don't know son, I'm still paying."

71. I used to be indecisive. Now I'm not sure.

72. You're never too old to learn something stupid.

73. Women may not hit harder, but they hit lower.

74. A bargain is something you don't need at a price you can't resist.

75. Jesus loves you, but everyone else thinks you're an asshole.

76. Knowledge is power, and power corrupts. So study hard and be evil.

77. When tempted to fight fire with fire, remember that the Fire Department usually uses water.

78. To be sure of hitting the target, shoot first and call whatever you hit the target.

79. You are such a good friend that if we were on a sinking ship together and there was only one life jacket... I'd miss you heaps and think of you often.

80. I like work. It fascinates me. I sit and look at it for hours.

81. A TV can insult your intelligence, but nothing rubs it in like a computer.

82. If at first you don't succeed, skydiving is not for you!

83. A bus is a vehicle that runs twice as fast when you are after it as when you are in it.

84. Some people hear voices.. Some see invisible people.. Others have no imagination whatsoever.

85. Virginity is like a soap-bubble, one prick and it is gone.

86. If winning isn't everything why do they keep score?

87. Whoever coined the phrase "Quiet as a mouse" has never stepped on one.

88. If you are supposed to learn from your mistakes, why do some people have more than one child.

89. Change is inevitable, except from a vending machine.

90. Why is it that most nudists are people you don't want to see naked?

91. I don't suffer from insanity. I enjoy every minute of it.

92. When you go into court, you are putting your fate into the hands of people who weren't smart enough to get out of jury duty.

93. If you keep your feet firmly on the ground, you'll have trouble putting on your pants.

94. Does this rag smell like chloroform to you?

95. What's the difference between a northern fairytale and a southern fairytale? A northern fairytale begins "Once upon a time…" A southern fairytale begins "Y'all ain't gonna believe this shit…"

96. You know the world is going crazy when the best rapper is a white guy, the best golfer is a black guy, the tallest guy in the NBA is Chinese, the Swiss hold the America's Cup, France is accusing the U.S. of arrogance, Germany doesn't want to go to war, and the three most powerful men in America are named 'Bush', 'Dick', and 'Colon'. Need I say more?

97. Children seldom misquote you. In fact, they usually repeat word for word what you shouldn't have said.

98. Good health is merely the slowest possible rate at which one can die.

99. Some mistakes are too much fun to only make once.

100. If Bill Gates had a penny for every time I had to reboot my computer…oh wait, he does.

101. The big difference between sex for money and sex for free is that sex for money usually costs a lot less.

102. I don't have an attitude problem. You have a perception problem. George Washington said "We would have a black president when pigs fly!"… well, swine flu.

103. Children in the dark make accidents, but accidents in the dark make children.

104. Life's a bitch, 'cause if it was a slut, it'd be easy.

105. I have never understood why women love cats. Cats are independent, they don't listen, they don't come in when you call, they like to stay out all night, and when they're home they like to be left alone and sleep. In other words, every quality that women hate in a man, they love in a cat.

106. You know your children are growing up when they stop asking you where they came from and refuse to tell you where they're going.

107. Deja Vu – When you think you're doing something you've done before, it's because God thought it was so funny, he had to rewind it for his friends.

108. The difference between an oral thermometer and a rectal thermometer is in the taste.

109. Girls are like roads, more the curves, more the dangerous they are.

110. Money talks…but all mine ever says is good-bye.

111. It is hard to understand how a cemetery raised its burial cost and blamed it on the cost of living.

112. By the time a man realises that his father was right, he has a son who thinks he's wrong.

113. By the time you learn the rules of life, you're too old to play the game.

114. Does time fly when you're having sex or was it really just one minute?

115. If you're looking for sympathy, you'll find it in the dictionary between "shit" and "syphilis"

116. Why do they lock gas station bathrooms? Are they afraid someone will clean them?

117. Keep the dream alive: Hit the snooze button.

118. I don't have a beer gut, I have a protective covering for my rock hard abs.

119. Build a man a fire, and he'll be warm for a day. Set a man on fire, and he'll be warm for the rest of his life.

120. Why is it called tourist season if we can't shoot them?

121. We have all heard that a million monkeys banging on a million typewriters will eventually reproduce the entire works of Shakespeare. Now, thanks to the Internet, we know this is not true.

122. Who was the first to see a cow and think "I wonder what will happen if I squeeze these dangly things and drink whatever comes out?"

123. Panties are not best thing on earth, but next to it.

124. Remember, if you smoke after sex you're doing it too fast.

125. Friends may come and go, but enemies accumulate.

126. The difference between in-laws and outlaws? Outlaws are wanted.

127. If you can stay calm while all around you is chaos, then you probably haven't completely understood the situation.

128. You know, they got a luggage store in the airport? A place to buy a piece of luggage? How late do you have to be for a flight where you're like, 'Fuck it – just grab a pile of shit. We'll get a bag at the airport'.

129. It's amazing that the amount of news that happens in the world everyday always just exactly fits the newspaper.

130. Hard work never killed anyone, but why take the chance?

131. Without nipples, breasts would be pointless.

132. According to a new survey, women say they feel more comfortable undressing in front of men than they do undressing in front of other women. They say that women are too judgmental, where, of course, men are just grateful.

133. I have all the money I'll ever need – if I die by 4:00 p.m. today.

134. Experience is what you get when you didn't get what you wanted.

135. Two years ago I married a lovely young virgin, and if that doesn't change soon, I'm gonna divorce her.

136. Dogs have masters. Cats have staff.

137. Isn't it odd the way everyone automatically assumes that the goo in soap dispensers is always soap? I like to fill mine with mustard, just to teach people a lesson in trust.

138. Well aren't you a waste of two billion years of evolution.

139. The right to be heard does not automatically include the right to be taken seriously.

140. When you choke a smurf, what color does it turn?

141. Archaeologist: someone whose career lies in ruins.

142. Join The Army, visit exotic places, meet strange people, then kill them.

143. Women should not have children after 35. Really… 35 children are enough.

144. Why do people keep running over a string a dozen times with their vacuum cleaner, then reach down, pick it up, examine it, then put it down to give their vacuum one more chance?

145. I don't have an attitude; I have a personality you can't handle.

146. I married Miss Right. I just didn't know her first name was Always.

147. The probability of someone watching you is proportional to the stupidity of your action.

148. Impotence: Nature's way of saying "No hard feelings".

149. Do you realize that in about 40 years, we'll have thousands of old ladies running around with tattoos?

150. There are three kinds of people: The ones who learn by reading. The ones who learn by observation. And the rest of them who have to touch the fire to learn it's hot.

151. We are all time travellers moving at the speed of exactly 60 minutes per hour

152. To err is human, to blame it on somebody else shows management potential.

153. Alcohol is a perfect solvent: It dissolves marriages, families and careers.

154. Only in America… do banks leave both doors open and then chain the pens to the counters.

155. Vegetarian: Native American definition for "lousy hunter".

156. Materialism: buying things we don't need with money we don't have to

impress people that don't matter.

157. The Miss Universe pageant is fixed. All the winners are from Earth.

158. It matters not whether you win or lose: what matters is whether I win or lose.

159. If you can't convince them, confuse them.

160. Don't piss me off! I'm running out of places to hide the bodies.

161. Progress is made by lazy men looking for an easier way to do things.

162. See, the problem is that God gives men a brain and a penis, and only enough blood to run one at a time.

163. I read recipes the same way I read science fiction. I get to the end and I think, "Well, that's not going to happen."

164. Smith & Wesson: The original point and click interface.

165. The difference between fiction and reality? Fiction has to make sense.

166. 100,000 sperm and you were the fastest?

167. I saw six men kicking and punching the mother-in-law. My neighbour said 'Are you going to help?' I said 'No, six should be enough.'

168. A friend is someone who will help you move. A GOOD friend is

someone who will help you move a dead body.

169. Why do we press harder on a remote control when we know the batteries are getting weak?

170. Clinton lied. A man might forget where he parks or where he lives, but he never forgets oral sex, no matter how bad it is.

171. What if there were no hypothetical questions?

172. For every action, there is a corresponding over-reaction.

173. I'm a humble person, really. I'm actually much greater than I think I am.

174. Why is it called Alcoholics ANONYMOUS when the first thing you do is stand up and say, 'My name is Peter and I am an alcoholic'

175. The best way to lie is to tell the truth, carefully edited truth.

176. Every day, man is making bigger and better fool-proof things, and every day, nature is making bigger and better fools. So far, I think nature is winning.

177. I don't have a solution, but I do admire the problem.

178. The hardest thing to learn in life is which bridge to cross and which to burn.

179. People tend to make rules for others and exceptions for themselves.

180. There are two kinds of friends: those who are around when you need them, and those who are around when they need you.

181. Don't steal. That's the government's job.

182. A celebrity is someone who works hard all his life to become known and then wears dark glasses to avoid being recognized.

183. IRS: We've got what it takes to take what you've got.

184. Stress is when you wake up screaming and you realize you haven't fallen asleep yet.

185. Sometimes the best helping hand you can give is a good, firm push.

186. What is the most important thing to learn in chemistry? Never lick the spoon.

187. Lite: the new way to spell "Light," now with 20% fewer letters!

188. Unless you're the lead dog, the view never changes.

189. A conscience is what hurts when all your other parts feel so good.

190. No one is listening until you fart.

191. Only dead fish go with the flow.

192. Why don't you slip into something more comfortable...like a coma.

193. Drink coffee! Do stupid things faster with more energy!

194. This isn't an office. It's hell with fluorescent lighting.

195. A positive attitude may not solve all your problems, but it will annoy enough people to make it worth the effort.

196. Why is it so hard for women to find men that are sensitive, caring, and good-looking? Because those men already have boyfriends.

197. Life is like a bird, it's pretty cute until it shits on your head.

198. I'm multi-talented: I can talk and piss you off at the same time.

199. The easiest job in the world has to be coroner. Surgery on dead people. What's the worst thing that could happen? If everything went wrong, maybe you'd get a pulse.

200. Foreign Aid: The transfer of money from poor people in rich countries to rich people in poor countries.

201. How do you get a sweet little 80-year-old lady to say the F word? Get another sweet little 80-year-old lady to yell *BINGO*!

202. 1 in 5 people in the world are Chinese. There are 5 people in my family, so it must be one of them. It's either my mum or my dad. Or my older brother Colin. Or my younger brother Ho-Cha-Chu. But I think it's

Colin.

203. If corn oil comes from corn, where does baby oil come from?

204. True friendship comes when the silence between two people is comfortable.

205. The trouble with being punctual is that nobody's there to appreciate it.

206. If I'd shot you sooner, I'd be out of jail by now.

207. Insanity is hereditary. You get it from your kids.

208. Everything is edible, some things are only edible once.

209. What has four legs and an arm? A happy pit bull.

210. If Wal-Mart is lowering prices every day, why isn't anything in the store free yet?

211. There are no winners in life...only survivors.

212. Politics is the art of looking for trouble, finding it, misdiagnosing it and then misapplying the wrong remedies.

213. Just about the time when you think you can make ends meet, somebody moves the ends.

214. Wise people think all they say, fools say all they think.

215. One tequila, two tequila, three tequila, floor.

216. The knack of flying is learning how to throw yourself at the ground and miss.

217. If you must choose between two evils, pick the one you've never tried before.

218. It's so simple to be wise. Just think of something stupid to say and then don't say it.

219. We are all part of the ultimate statistic – ten out of ten die.

220. Hippopotomonstrosesquippedaliophobia: Fear of long words.

221. A committee is twelve men doing the work of one.

222. Ever notice that people who spend money on beer, cigarettes, and lottery tickets are always complaining about being broke and not feeling well?

223. If everything seems to be coming your way, you're probably in the wrong lane.

224. I'm in shape. Round is a shape isn't it

225. When we were together, you always said you'd die for me. Now that we've broke up, I think it's time you kept your promise!

226. She said she was approaching forty, and I couldn't help wondering from what direction.

227. If your dog is barking at the back door and your wife is yelling at the front door, who do you let in first? The dog, of course. He'll shut up once you let him in.

228. During sex, my girlfriend always wants to talk to me. Just the other night she called me from a hotel.

229. They keep saying the right person will come along, I think mine got hit by a truck.

230. I said "no" to drugs, but they just wouldn't listen.

231. Alcoholism is the only disease that tries to convince you that you don't have it.

232. I sometimes go to my own little world, but that's okay, they know me there.

233. I like long walks, especially when they are taken by people who annoy me.

234. My drinking team has a bowling problem.

235. A fine is a tax for doing wrong. A tax is a fine for doing well.

236. Why do they use sterilized needles for death by lethal injection?

237. It's not how good your work is, it's how well you explain it.

238. Seen it all, done it all, can't remember most of it.

239. I wanna hang a map of the world in my house. Then I'm gonna put pins into all the locations that I've traveled to. But first, I'm gonna have to travel to the top two corners of the map so it won't fall down.

240. Losing a husband can be hard: in my case it was almost impossible.

241. Efficiency is a highly developed form of laziness.

242. If a turtle doesn't have a shell, is he homeless or naked?

243. Anyone who has never made a mistake has never tried anything new.

244. Failure is not falling down, it is not getting up again.

245. Bills travel through the mail at twice the speed

246. The best thing about living at the beach is that you only have assholes on three sides of you.

247. Silence doesn't mean your sexual performance left her speechless.

248. The farther away the future is, the better it looks.

249. Never test the depth of the water with both feet.

250. Did you hear about the guy whose whole left side was cut off? He's all right now.

251. I have to exercise early in the morning before my brain figures out what I'm doing.

252. Some of us learn from the mistakes of others; the rest of us have to be the others.

253. Every so often, I like to go to the window, look up, and smile for a satellite picture.

254. At every party there are two kinds of people: those who want to go home and those who don't. The trouble is, they are usually married to each other.

255. The journey of a thousand miles begins with a broken fan belt and a flat tire.

256. Constipated people don't give a crap.

257. Why is a bra singular and panties plural?

258. Be safety conscious. 80% of people are caused by accidents.

259. Without ME, it's just AWESO.

260. I was thinking about how people seem to read the Bible a whole lot more as they get older. Then it dawned on me... they were cramming for

their finals.

261. Be careful of your thoughts, they may become words at any moment.

262. If you don't care where you are, then you ain't lost.

263. You can easily judge the character of a man by how he treats those who can do nothing for him.

264. I pretend to work as long as they pretend to pay me.

265. You ever make fun of someone so much, you think you should thank them for all the good times you've had?

266. You have two choices in life: You can stay single and be miserable, or get married and wish you were dead.

267. I am not a vegetarian because I love animals. I am a vegetarian because I hate plants.

268. Ham and Eggs: A day's work for a chicken, a lifetime commitment for a pig.

269. If the number 2 pencil is the most popular, why is it still number 2?

270. Don't hate me because I'm beautiful. Hate me because your boyfriend thinks so.

271. Everyone has the right to be stupid, but you are abusing the privilege!

272. The trouble with doing something right the first time is that nobody appreciates how difficult it was.

273. The human brain is a wonderful thing. It starts working the moment you are born, and never stops until you stand up to speak in public.

274. Do not walk behind me, for I may not lead. Do not walk ahead of me, for I may not follow. Do not walk beside me either. Just pretty much leave me the hell alone.

275. Rap is to music as Etch-A-Sketch is to art.

276. Men are like mascara, they usually run at the first sign of emotion.

277. Trust but verify.

278. The difference between divorce and legal separation is that a legal separation gives a husband time to hide his money.

279. WARNING: The consumption of alcohol may cause you to think you can sing.

280. The last time I was inside a woman was when I went to the Statue of Liberty.

281. Why do women always ask questions that have no right answers?

282. I ran into my ex the other day, hit reverse, and ran into him again.

283. How do you get holy water? Boil the hell out of it.

284. I'd kill for a Nobel Peace Prize.

285. Why do you need a driver's license to buy liquor when you can't drink and drive?

286. Sometimes when I reflect back on all the beer I drink I feel shamed. Then I look into the glass and think about the workers in the brewery and all of their hopes and dreams. If I didn't drink this beer, they might be out of work and their dreams would be shattered. Then I say to myself, "It is better that I drink this beer and let their dreams come true than be selfish and worry about my liver.

287. Insanity is defined as doing the same thing over and over again, expecting different results.

288. Think of how stupid the average person is, and realize half of them are stupider than that.

289. It was love at first sight. Then I took a second look !!

290. I think, therefore I'm single.

291. It ain't the jeans that make your butt look fat.

292. Should crematoriums give discounts for burn victims?

293. When you stop believing in Santa Claus is when you start getting

clothes for Christmas!

294. I bet you I could stop gambling.

295. Two antennas met on a roof, fell in love and got married. The ceremony wasn't much, but the reception was excellent.

296. If a dog sniffs your ass, you're probably a bitch.

297. Never agree to plastic surgery if the doctor's office is full of portraits by Picasso.

298. 668 – The neighbour of the beast.

299. Sex at age 90 is like trying to shoot pool with a rope.

300. Children in the back seats of cars cause accidents, but accidents in the back seats of cars cause children.

301. I've learned that the people you care most about in life are taken from you too soon and all the less important ones just never go away.

302. Squirrels – nature's speed bumps.

303. It's bad luck to be superstitious.

304. There are two kinds of people who don't say much: those who are quiet and those who talk a lot.

305. The reason grandchildren and grandparents get along so well is because they have a common "enemy".

306. With a calendar, your days are numbered.

307. If it's true that we are here to help others, then what exactly are the others here for?

308. It's not the bullet that kills you, it's the hole.

309. If good things come in small packages, then more good things can come in large packages.

310. You may have a heart of gold, but so does a hard-boiled egg.

311. My wife ran off with my best friend last week. I miss him!

312. A woman has got to love a bad man once or twice in her life, to be thankful for a good one.

313. A cat, by any other name, is still a sneaky little furball that barfs on the furniture.

314. Laugh and the world laughs with you. Snore and you sleep alone

315. Married men live longer than single men, but they're a lot more willing to die.

316. If life hands you lemons, break out the tequila!

317. Beauty is only skin deep…but ugly goes all the way to the bone!

318. A cheap shot is a terrible thing to waste.

319. A hard thing about a business is minding your own.

320. Most women don't know where to look when they're eating a banana.

321. My wife and I were happy for twenty years… and then we met.

322. I saw a sign that said "Watch for children" and I thought… "that sounds like a fair trade."

323. Whiteboards are remarkable.

324. Outside of a dog, a book is man's best friend… inside of a dog, it's too dark to read.

325. I wonder what "don't touch" is in Braille.

326. If at first you don't succeed, destroy all evidence that you tried.

327. I refused to believe my road-worker father was stealing from his job, but when I got home, all the signs were there.

328. My grandfather has the heart of a lion and a lifetime ban from the local zoo.

329. My ex owned a parakeet and OMG that thing would never shut up... but the bird was cool

330. I recently decided to sell my vacuum cleaner, all it was doing was gathering dust.

331. The first time I got a universal remote control, I thought to myself... "This changes everything."

332. I haven't slept for three days... because that would be too long.

333. The new corduroy pillows are making headlines.

334. I wanted to write a joke about feminism, but my husband wouldn't let me.

335. There's a fine line between numerator and denominator.

336. I bought a dog from a blacksmith and when I got him home, he made a bolt for the door.

337. Time flies like an arrow, fruit flies like a banana.

338. I tried making a pencil with an eraser at both ends, but then I realized it was pointless.

339. Childhood is like being drunk, everyone remembers what you did, except you.

340. I saw a TV for sale in a shop window and the sign said "TV cheap, broken volume knob"...and I thought to myself "Wow, I can't turn that down!"

341. When your only tool is a hammer, all problems start looking like nails.

342. 99 percent of lawyers give the rest a bad name.

343. The only substitute for good manners is fast reflexes.

344. Support bacteria - they're the only culture some people have.

345. Letting the cat out of the bag is a whole lot easier than putting it back in.

346. Well, here I am! What are your other two wishes?

347. Sounds like its time to get that Enterprise built!

348. Time doesn't exist. Clocks exist.

349. My mind's made up, don't confuse me with facts.

350. Talk is cheap. Until you hire a lawyer.

351. Take my advice — I'm not using it.

352. I got lost in thoughts. It was unfamiliar territory.

353. Sure, I'd love to help you out ... now, which way did you come in?

354. I started with nothing, and I still have most of it.

355. Ever stop to think, and forget to start again?

356. There is no dance without the dancers.

357. Out of my mind. Back in five minutes.

358. The problem with trouble shooting is that trouble shoots back.

359. If you are here - who is running hell?

360. If nothing was learned, nothing was taught.

361. The dogs bark but the caravan moves on.

362. Which one of these is the non-smoking lifeboat?

363. Treat each day as your last; one day you will be right.

364. Red meat is not bad for you. Fuzzy green meat is bad for you.

365. Isn't it scary that doctors call what they do "practice"?

366. The problem with sex in the movies is, that the popcorn usually spills.

367. If I want your opinion, I'll ask you to fill out the necessary forms.

368. Living on Earth is expensive, but it does include a free trip around the sun.

369. Despite the cost of living, have you noticed how popular it remains?

370. Always remember you're unique, just like everyone else.

371. Everybody repeat after me: "We are all individuals."

372. Confession is good for the soul, but bad for your career.

373. A bartender is just a pharmacist with a limited inventory.

374. I want patience - AND I WANT IT NOW!!!!

375. A day for firm decisions! Or is it?

376. Am I ambivalent? Well, yes and no.

377. Bombs don't kill people, explosions kill people.

378. How many of you believe in telekinesis? Raise MY hand!

379. Every organisation is perfectly designed to get the results they are getting.

380. Welcome to Utah: set your watch back 20 years.

381. Under my gruff exterior lies an even gruffer interior.

382. Failure is not an option. It's bundled with your software.

383. I think sex is better than logic, but I can't prove it.

384. If at first you don't succeed, redefine success.

385. I want to go to IKEA, hide in a wardrobe, wait for someone to open it and yell "WELCOME TO NARNIA".

386. Life isn't about waiting for the storm to pass ... it's about learning to dance in the rain!

387. My conscience is clean — I have never used it.

388. Sugar - Honey - Iced - Tea ... Guess what it means.

389. Friday is my second favourite F word.

390. The only thing I hate more than having a dirty house is cleaning.

391. The reason why I hate mornings so much is that they start while I'm still sleeping.

392. Every one of us has a friend, who says he'll be in 5 minutes, but comes in two hours.

393. Brains are wonderful, I wish everyone had one.

394. Nothing spoils the target more than a hit.

395. A person has to have a warm heart and a cold beer.

396. A warning shot into the head.

397. Only an ass can be divided in half.

398. If you want to hide your face, go out naked.

399. The panic begins with the first one to say 'Calm down!'

400. The device will work much better, if you turn it on.

401. To the question 'What are you doing here?' 72% answered negative.

402. Approach, stick, and get infected.

403. One head is ok, but a whole body is much better.

404. If you can't buy a person, you can always sell him.

405. To start from zero, you need to crawl up to it.

406. Nothing brings neighbors together, like a broken elevator.

407. An idea came to the mind, and now she's searching for the brain.

408. Yesterday, I fell down from a 10 meter ladder. Thank God I was on the third step.

409. Only newlyweds and liars have sex every day.

410. Ask the horse, he has a bigger head.

411. Do you need space? Join NASA!

412. I don't think you are stupid. You just have a bad luck when thinking

413. Life is beautiful… from Friday to Monday.

414. The most important stakeholder in you life is You.

415. Marriage is the main reason for divorce.

416. As a CEO of a newly established start-up I slept like a baby: waking up every two hours and crying.

417. Group projects in school make me understand why Batman prefers working alone.

418. This is a real truth: You never realize what you have until it's gone. Toilet paper, for example.

419. If you want girls to be running after you – become a bus driver.

420. Someday your car indicated how much you earned, but now it shows how much you owe.

421. One day I shall solve my problems with maturity. Today, however, it

will be a box of beer.

422. I wanted to get rid of 6 pounds during the summer. I'm only 7.5 pounds away from my goal.

423. Read through the label of ingredients of your food and then you" understand why it's important to pray before you eat.

424. Today I have texted my friends: "hey, I've lost my phone somewhere, may you give me a call?". 12 friends called me. I think I need to start looking for more intelligent friends.

425. Don't worry, computer, even I go to sleep after 30 minutes of inactivity.

426. Pregnancy is a gift, but you have to wait for 9 months to see it.

427. When I get naked in the bathroom, the shower gets turned on.

428. I was lying in bed today when somebody knocked on my door. I opened the door and found my neighbor, asking for a small donation for the local swimming pool. I gave him a bottle of water.

429. Everybody would agree that we should put an extra day between Saturday and Sunday.

430. I'm not fat, I'm easier to see.

431. Have you noticed that in cartoons gravity does not work until you look

down.

432. Sometimes it is worth lending $10 for someone, who you don't want to see anymore.

433. If you really love someone – you have to set them free. If they come back to you, it probably means nobody else liked them. Thus, set them free again.

434. The best thing to decrease your wrinkles is Photoshop.

435. God sees everything. Your neighbors – even more.

436. Today I saw something which reminded me of you. But never mind, I flushed it down and it all went great after that.

437. Million dollar idea – invest a billion $ into Twitter.

438. If your offer is still valid, then I want to refuse it once more.

439. The IQ test showed that she is extremely beautiful.

440. If you want to help your kid start speaking earlier – put him in a hot bath.

441. If you want to earn money with the help of Facebook – go to its settings, delete your account and start working.

442. Success is like pregnancy – everyone congratulates you but they don't

know how many times you had to f**k to achieve it.

443. If you're lost in woods and have no compass, wait for the autumn – birds will fly to the south.

444. This happens for everyone – when you don't know how to spell a word, you think of a whole new sentence to avoid using it.

445. Everybody knows that feeling when you check your phone to see what time it is now and then have to check it again because the first time you weren't paying attention.

446. If you take a 4 million dollar loan, you will be paying it back for 40 years. But if you steel 4 million dollars, you get to prison for 7 years only. This thought doesn't allow me to fall asleep.

447. I earn a lot, but get little.

448. Optimism – is a lack of information.

449. Remember good times… when phones were stupid and people were smart.

450. Just where the tracks of failure end, the fence of the graveyard begins.

451. Liar's legs are short, but well trained…

452. A cooler is also a helicopter. Only a small one.

453. If the parachute didn't open, don't jump for the second time.

454. If a person opens his mouth and says nothing, it means he's eating.

455. There are 7 days in a week, but no fun at all.

456. If an apple has fallen on you, you should get out of there; the apple doesn't fall far from the tree.

457. Stop the world, I want to get out!

458. Where does Thursday come before Wednesday? In the dictionary.

459. You don't notice the air, until someone spoils it.

460. Don't drink while driving – you will spill the beer.

461. If you love a woman, you shouldn't be ashamed to show her to your wife.

462. Life didn't work out, but everything else is not that bad.

463. If someone notices you with an open zipper, answer proudly: professional habit.

464. If you're not supposed to eat at night, why is there a light bulb in the refrigerator?

465. There is a new trend in our office; everyone is putting names on their

food. I saw it today, while I was eating a sandwich named Kevin.

466. The speed of light is when you take out a bottle of beer out of the fridge before the light comes on.

467. To weigh 50 kilos and say that you're fat, that is so female…

468. Did you know that your body is made 70% of water? And now I'm thirsty.

469. When people come up to me and ask why I don't have any tattoos I reply: would you put a bumper sticker on a Ferrari?

470. Men are born between women legs and that is the reason why they are trying to get back there the rest of their life.

471. Men live better than women. First of all, they get married later and secondly, they die earlier.

472. Transitional age is when during a hot day you don't know what you want – ice cream or beer.

473. There are two types of guys: those who pee in the shower and those who don't admit it.

474. He is crazy and when you think that you have reached the bottom of this craziness, you suddenly find out there's a crazy underground garage, 8 floors underneath.

475. A healthy male organism is the one, which wakes up in the morning before the man.

476. It is said that, a way to a man's heart goes through a stomach. Aha…you might think that men go to their lovers to eat some soup

477. Men are like Bluetooth. When they're close – they're connected, when they move further – they start looking for new equipment.

478. If a man goes left (cheats) for four times, according to the rules of geometry, he will come home.

479. When looking at a woman an old man remembers, the young one – wishes.

480. Moses was leading his people through the desert for 40 years. It seems, even in Biblical times men avoided asking the way.

481. Real men don't cry…tears for real men are only unnecessary liquids in the body.

482. A wife can enjoy anything, until it's not my salary.

483. You need to carry women in your arms; they will climb on your back by themselves.

484. Darling, what are you thinking about right now? If I would want you to know, I would say it not think about it.

485. It's not a flaw to have a husband, but an essential drawback to have a wife.

486. If at first you don't succeed, try doing it in the way your wife told you to. You'll be amazed.

487. Husbands never have cash – they are married.

488. The salary of wife is HER salary. The salary of husband is family's budget.

489. If a woman is cold as a fish, a man has to be as patient as a fisherman.

490. The end of a relationship isn't the worst thing. It's worse when it doesn't end after the end.

491. My ex wrote to me: Can you delete my number? I responded: Who is this?

492. I never could bring a woman into my house. At first, because of the parents. Later, because of the wife.

493. I can only stand a woman being by my side from sundown to sunrise.

494. There is nothing worse than cheating on a woman. But nothing is more enjoyable if you succeed.

495. You can't choose the right key to a woman's heart? Try choosing for some other place.

496. If it's getting cramped in the closet, you should look for a new hiding place.

497. A man is someone who would die for his woman, rather than live with her.

498. If you want to be TOGETHER, you have TO-GET-HER.

499. A woman is hiding her past from a man. A man is hiding her future.

500. How can men and women understand each other when they want different things? A man needs a woman and a woman needs a man.

501. Women never forget men that they were happy with, men – women that they failed to have.

502. We should carry women in our hands, but often they climb on our head.

503. Men always go to the left because women are always right.

504. When a woman says that she'll be ready in 10 minutes, she is using the same time-scale as a man, when he is saying that the game will be over in 10 minutes.

505. Don't worry if you had a bad day – just remember, that some people have the name of their Ex's tattooed on their body.

506. When a woman falls in love, no-one knows that, except herself. When

a man falls in love, everybody knows it, except her.

507. If you are having a dispute with a woman and you hear her saying "WOW" – you should run.

508. A four letter word that every man is afraid of? (More)

509. Mostly men lie before the elections, sex and after fishing.

510. It's uncomfortable when the neighbor's kids look like you.

511. Men are like frogs, the most important thing is to jump on faster.

512. Men should be like coffee: strong, hot and not letting you sleep for the whole night. However, most of them are like copy machines: suitable only for reproduction.

513. Men mostly hate two words: 'not' and 'enough'… unless you say them together.

514. Have a girl that everyone else dreams about, but don't dream about a girl that everyone else has.

515. Of course, women are meant to drive. Why else would they place three mirrors in the car.

516. If a man gives you flowers without any reason, it means there is a reason.

517. What if there were no men in the world? There would be lots of happy and fat women!

518. Why does everyone say that women love money? They don't, look how fast they spend it.

519. Women are very good! They can forgive a man…even if he's not guilty.

520. Female logics: I'm sad. I will buy something I don't even need.

521. Women go on a diet on 3 occasions: 1. When they break up with a guy; 2. When they meet a guy; 3. On Mondays.

522. Darling, you are the most beautiful woman in this party! Did you invite these guests on purpose?

523. A beautiful woman delights a man's eye, an ugly – woman's eye.

524. All the women are the same, only some of them don't show it.

525. Don't look for a perfect woman – today I will be at home…

526. Is the day that you do laundry, cook, clean, iron and so on, is also called day off?

527. In the competition of female logic, a random number generator won.

528. What's the difference between a fiancée and a wife? Approximately 15

kilos.

529. The value of money in a relationship: the 10 bucks that the wife and the tax inspection don't know about are worth more than the 100 that both know about.

530. You should argue with your wife only when she's not around.

531. A wife is like a boomerang – the harder you throw the faster she comes back.

532. When you want to marry a beautiful, a smart and a rich woman – marry three times.

533. If a wife is silent and not arguing – it means she's sleeping.

534. A woman is like a suitcase: both hard to carry and a pity to throw away.

535. A woman is like a shadow: when you walk from behind she runs away. When you run from her – follows you behind.

536. Before the wedding I have loved all the women on earth, after the wedding one woman less.

537. A woman is like a parachute – can refuse at any time, that's why you need to have a spare one.

538. You need to love a woman, not try to understand her.

539. A battle of opposites... A man wants to go to sleep fast and silent... A woman wants to talk loud and long half of the night.

540. I have two questions for you: No. 1. Is where have you been all my life? And the second one – would you please go back there?

541. Mosquitoes have more humanity than some women: they drink your blood silently

542. A stupid woman holds her man by the throat, a clever one – the hand, and the wise one – doesn't hold at all.

543. Dear men, have you noticed, that no women ever started an argument with a man when he was cleaning the dishes, vacuuming the carpet or dusting...

544. Do you know one sentence that makes you remember all the bad things that you've done in your life? That is "I need to talk to you".

545. A woman may perform orgasm. And men can perform relationship

546. Just because I'm smiling, it doesn't mean that I would not love to hit you in the face.

547. A woman is like a well-served table at which a man looks one way before he eats and differently after he ate.

548. Women need a reason to have sex. Men just need a place.

549. If you consider women to be the weak gender, try to pull the blanket from her in the night-time.

550. How to make a woman nervous in just a couple of seconds? Take a picture of her and... do not show it to her.

551. Women never notice what we do for them, but they always notice, what we don't.

552. Talking about girls is like talking about the dead – good or nothing.

553. Women are smarter than men; they know less but understand more.

554. There is one thing that men and women agree on: they all don't trust women.

555. Confucius says Love one another. If it doesn't work, just interchange the last two words.

556. There are two ways to control a woman, but no one knows them...

557. The smartest woman is the one that lets the man act as he wants – stupidly.

558. Woman – a complete opposite of a dog. A dog understands everything but can't say anything.

559. In the beginning, God created the earth. He rested. Then he created a man. He rested. Then God created a woman. Neither God nor man rested

from that day.

560. A woman behind a steering wheel – is like a monkey with a grenade.

561. When woman says "do whatever you want" that actually means "do not do whatever you want".

562. I tried searching on Google to find out what do women want. But Google result was: "We are searching too"…

563. The line between wrong and right is as wide as the thread from a spider's web…

564. A women gets angry when her friend eats as much but stays slim.

565. The logics of a woman: I called myself the beast. Now he should say a compliment.

566. It's easy to make a woman happy – just not that cheap.

567. If women didn't exist, all the money in the world wouldn't make sense.

568. Arguing with a woman – is like a visit to the dentist: very painful or very expensive.

569. A woman is helpless until the nail polish is dry.

570. God created a man, and then he thought he could do better and created a woman.

571. Beautiful woman is a weapon, but if she's also clever, that's a bomb.

572. How come a woman eats 1 kilo sweets and is able to gain 5 kilos overweight.

573. Do you think that every girl's dream is to find the perfect guy? Come on, please, every girl's dream is to get thin by eating cakes.

574. What is 90-60-90? Driving past the cops in the city.

575. There are two types of pedestrians: quick and dead.

576. Driver, be careful of the places where children appear from!

577. Don't trust the traffic light; believe in the car heading towards you.

578. A sticker on the bumper: Drive on the footpath – there are too many idiots on the road.

579. Pedestrian is always right. While he's alive.

580. There is all the information you need in the road map, just not how to fold it back again.

581. There is no point of running away from a sniper. You will die from exhaustion.

582. There are lots of good people, but much less of useful ones.

583. There's good climate in heaven, but a better company in hell.

584. So there would be something to be silent about, there is always something to talk about.

585. 'A pedigree bulldog missing. Founders – rest in peace.'

586. Scientists proved that cows don't give us meat and milk. We just take it from them!

587. Women and cats will do as they want, and men and dogs should relax and get used to the idea.

588. Why are the camera lens circular and the photos rectangular?

589. Daddy, daddy! What does 'Format C: complete' means?

590. Windows 8 install program: computer not detected.

591. Do you know that every time you push a key on your computer, you kill more than a thousand microbes?

592. People can be divided into two categories: the first category doesn't know who Bill Gates is; the second one doesn't love him.

593. The more I get to know people, the more I start loving computers.

594. Do you want to change your life completely? Don't pay for the Internet.

595. Not everything is Windows that hangs...

596. To be wrong is human, to blame your computer — is even more human.

597. Soon, Windows pack will contain a tube of Colgate toothpaste.

598. Spelling mistakes are never visible before you push 'send'.

599. Who the hell is 'General Failure' and why is he reading my hard drive?

600. A well captured patient doesn't need anaesthetics.

601. Shut up — your dental filling will fall out.

602. All diseases are from stress, only syphilis from pleasure.

603. I don't drink, don't smoke, and don't hang out with guys. I go to bed at 10 p.m. and wake up at 6 a.m. But everything will change when I get out of prison.

604. You have to admit that Mondays aren't that bad, it's probably your job that sucks.

605. In every company there is an askhole — a person who constantly asks for your advice, yet always does the opposite.

606. If you came to work late, you should at least try to leave it earlier.

607. I need a six month vacation, twice a year.

608. Sometimes I write down my tasks that I have already done just to get the satisfactions of crossing them off.

609. Most of the people dream of not working and having lots of money. During an economic crisis 50 % of those dreams came true.

610. Team work is important; it helps to put the blame on someone else.

611. You don't work – you don't have money to live, you work – there's no time to live.

612. When there are no volunteers, they get appointed.

613. Life is scary; at least the salary is funny.

614. It doesn't matter how much you work, there will always be an asshole that works less but gets more.

615. If you have worked and didn't get anything, it means someone else got it.

616. Salary is like a period – you wait for it a whole month and it ends in a week.

617. I work to buy a car to go to work.

618. People say nothing's impossible, but I do nothing every day.

619. One cigarette shortens your life by two hours, one bottle of vodka by three hours, and a workday – eight hours.

620. Don't postpone something that your co-worker can do today.

621. Nothing ruins a Friday more than an understanding that today is Tuesday…

622. Morning is the time when everyone is jealous of unemployed.

623. If Monday was a person, he would be the most hated person in the world.

624. Who knows – does, who doesn't know – teaches, who doesn't know how to teach – leads.

625. If your job is to tell me how to do my job, then you should at least know what job I'm doing.

626. It's nice to fly sober, but unusual – the pilot said.

627. The garbage disposal company provides a new service – guarantee. If the client is not satisfied – the garbage will be returned double.

628. Scientists have proven that people will believe in anything that starts with the words 'scientists have proven'.

629. Patient, wake up! It's time to drink your sleeping pills.

630. After listening to my story, my psychiatrist registered to his one psychiatrist.

631. When things don't work out for you right away, just remember that it takes 6 months to build a Bentley car, and 13 hours to build a Toyota.

632. If you give a student the base, he will fall asleep.

633. If you are doing math and you think it's easy, then you are doing it wrong.

634. If you could choose between the World Peace and Bill Gates' money, what color would be your Ferrari?

635. Money comes and goes, and goes, and goes…

636. If you're rich, I'm single.

637. ATM showed: 'Insufficient funds'. And I thought – me or the bank?

638. Don't steal, government hates competition.

639. If you think that the government doesn't care about you, try at least once not to pay your taxes!

640. When we break the law we pay fines, when we act right we pay taxes.

641. I'm selling a parachute – just as new, used only one time, didn't open once.

642. An advertisement states: telepath needed. You know where to apply.

643. A shampoo commercial: My hair was dry and dead before and now it's wet and moves.

644. An ad at the zoo: 'Don't scare the ostriches! The floors are concrete!'

645. 'And how will you prove your love?' 'Darling, accept it as an axiom.'

646. Paid love costs less.

647. Love is like peeing yourself – everyone can see but only you feel the warmth.

648. Three things for you to do today: (1) dig a hole; (2) name it love; (3) watch till someone falls in love.

649. When someone tells you that nothing can be more complicated than love, throw engineering books on their face.

650. I would press pause on fifa for you.

651. I love being married. It's so great to find one special person you want to annoy for the rest of your life.

652. God gave us the brain to work out problems. However, we use it to create more problems.

653. The light at the end of the tunnel – are the front lights of a train.

654. If the fortune has turned her back on you, you can do whatever you want behind her back.

655. It is said that, you can't buy happiness. You only need to know the right places…

656. Some people are so poor, all they have is money.

657. It's just a bad day, not a bad life.

658. Time you enjoy wasting, was not wasted

659. A man is mature when he can smile for the one, who offended him.

660. The older you get, the better you get, unless you are an apple.

661. If you think you are too small to make an impact on something, try to going bed with a mosquito in the room.

662. When was the last time that you did something for the first time?

663. Don't hurry to your funeral. They won't start without you.

664. Because of the defect in a parachute there is one person less on earth. In the case of the condom defect – one person more.

665. Why do people keep banging their heads into the wall? Corners are more effective!

666. It appeared that the light at the end of the tunnel was coming from a sign 'No exit'.

667. When the ship is sinking, the simplest thing is to call it a submarine.

668. It doesn't matter how big the choice of food is, still the same product always leaves our system.

669. To feel the pleasure of flight you don't need a parachute, you only need it if you want to feel it again.

670. Why the truth does always come out? Because most of the time the truth is a complete shit.

671. Not everything is gold that shines, but everything that smells shit – is definitely shit!

672. A person can do anything – until he starts doing something.

673. A conclusion is simply the place where you got tired of thinking.

674. When you're stressed, you eat Ice cream, chocolate and sweets. Do you know why? Because the word "stressed" spelled backwards is "desserts".

675. Sometimes I think that my brain is like a Bermuda Triangle – information goes inside but gets lost and is never found ever again.

676. Humans are the only species, who cut trees, make paper from it and then write on this paper "Save the trees".

677. It is good when a dog is your friend, but when your friend is a dog…

678. 'Are you threatening me?' 'It depends, if you got scared – yes I am; if not – I'm only warning you…'

679. Maybe you need a ladder to climb out of my business?

680. I like the sound of you not talking.

681. I'm not a Facebook status, you don't have to like me.

682. I found your nose in my business again.

683. How a true friend would help you keep your diet? He'd come and eat everything from your fridge.

684. I love watching fails compilations online – they remind me of you.

685. Second marriage is the victory of faith against the sane mind…

686. Do you know why the bride is wearing white at the wedding and the groom – black? It symbolizes the victory of good over the evil.

687. Marriage gives an opportunity to solve problems together, which you wouldn't have alone.

688. I divorced my wife because she used to spend all of my money. Now that I live alone, I can't understand where she used to get that money from.

689. T o get married at 21 is the same as to leave a party at 21:30.

690. I don't understand why should I get married and make one girl very happy, if I can stay a bachelor and make hundreds of them happy.

691. We now live in a house full of monsters that we have made ourselves...

692. A woman to a man during a slow dance: Is there a gun in your pocket or you're just happy that we met?

693. Remember, if a girl gave you a key to her heart; don't be so lucky, tomorrow she will change the locks.

694. When your ex says "you'll never find anyone like me" reply with "that's the point"

695. Game over. Thank you for playing.

696. When he offered her to be his girlfriend, she felt from a chair and was running around the room from happiness. And she replied: I will think about that.

697. Childs experience: if a mother is laughing at the fathers jokes, it means they have guests.

698. Because of the disregard towards safety techniques people not only die but are also born.

699. What is the difference between an old tire and 365 used condoms? None, it was a GOOD YEAR.

700. Happiness is a good health and a bad memory.

701. Reset – is not a button, but a cruel necessity…

702. Question: do you have children? 3 possible answers: yes, no, I don't know.

703. Let there be more gay people in the world! Because then there'll be more women left for us!

704. Sex is math – minus pants, divide the legs and multiply and multiply, just don't forget to extract the root on time so that there would be no residue left.

705. Shut up when you talk to me!

706. A relationship without trust is like having a mobile phone with no service. And what you do with a phone with no service? You play games.

707. Why is the day that you do laundry, cook, clean, iron and so on, called a day off?

708. You only see that the money is not the most important thing in life when you have it.

709. The pleasures of life can be both innocent and guilty.

710. The lessons of life are free, but they cost a lot.

711. Some people think that their life experience compensates for their lack of brain.

712. The more you plan, the less you have time to enjoy the life itself.

713. I will have enough money for the rest of my life. Of course, if I don't buy and eat anything.

714. If you want to change your life significantly just walk to the Mercedes-Benz 600 standing at the junction, take a brick and throw it into the windshield.

715. A human is afraid of two things: to live and to die. He gets used to everything else gradually.

716. Once in a while, something fails to fail, and we call it success.

717. Life is a race where everyone is trying to lead so that they would finish last.

718. Sometimes bad things happen to good people. However, in your case, it was definitely karma.

719. If you tried, but failed – hide all evidences of that.

720. I don't want to go to heaven after my death – there won't be any of my friends.

721. The most effective cleaning time is 15 minutes period between your friend's call and his visit to your house.

722. Liking your own status is like high fiving yourself in public

723. No genius would ever say he is a genius. I know this myself.

724. My mom always told me – if you can't say anything nice, then don't say anything at all. And some people wonder why I'm so quite around them.

725. I am an absolute master of doing the right things absolutely wrong.

726. The door to the other world is the window on the 18th floor.

727. The last one laughing is the one who shoots first.

728. The most popular last words:
    1. 'Don't worry, it's not loaded.'
    2. 'What will happen if we join these two wires?'

729. Murdered while trying to commit suicide.

730. Carry the charges carefully: it's better to be seen than to be remembered.

731. 'So far, everything seems to be normal' a man jumping from the 10th floor was thinking while flying through the third floor.

732. If you don't have any problems – it means you're dead.

733. One head is good. Two – already ugly.

734. At the zoo: 'Mom, is this a monkey?' 'No, it's only the cashier.'

735. Nothing suits a girl more than simplicity and see-through clothes.

736. There's nothing more beautiful in nature as a woman…And nothing more horrible than 'men' trying to imitate them.

737. Trying to choose the perfect dress for one night can destroy an entire room.

738. Golden rule: it's better to arrive late than to arrive ugly or smelly.

739. The alarm is on in the morning not because the windshield is busted, but the windshield is busted because the alarm is on in the morning.

740. Insomnia is not a problem; a problem is when you don't know why you get up in the morning.

741. God created the sleep, and the devil created an alarm clock.

742. The one, who snores, is the first one to fall asleep.

743. If I offer her to sleep over, she might misunderstand. And she will be right.

744. The most obvious thing people keep repeating: every night they go to sleep late and in the morning they feel like that was a bad idea.

745. Today I woke up and realized three horrible facts: Today is not Friday; Tomorrow is not Friday either; And even the day after tomorrow is not Friday.

746. It's easier to stay awake until 7 AM, than to wake-up at 7 AM!

747. If each day is a gift, I'd like to know where I can return Mondays.

748. I woke up in the morning; lay in my bed waiting until my mom will prepare the breakfast. And suddenly I remember that I'm the mom.

749. It's not "Tuesday", it's "ThreeDaysBeforeFriday".

750. After "Monday" and "Tuesday" even the calendar says "WTF".

751. Smile and life will kick your teeth out!

752. The one who smiles like a horse – smiles the best.

753. My advice is: smile, it confuses people.

754. 1/7 of our lives are Mondays.

755. Nerve cells born and die, and fat cells – live forever!

756. The longer the diagnosis, the shorter is the life left to live.

757. Death takes away the best people. It means that I will live long and long.

758. Anniversary is when there are lots of flowers and you are still alive.

759. If the music is too loud – most probably you're too old.

760. Shit happens, just flush it down and move on.

761. Life is short. Smile while you still have teeth.

762. It's Friday today and all I have planned for tonight is drinking and drinking. Oh and, did I mention drinking?

763. The older you get, the better you get, unless you are a banana.

764. If life dropped you a lemon, look for salt and tequila.

765. I want to die peacefully in my sleep, like my grandfather.. Not screaming and yelling like the passengers in his car.

766. When wearing a bikini, women reveal 90 % of their body... men are so polite they only look at the covered parts.

767. A straight face and a sincere-sounding "Huh?" have gotten me out of more trouble than I can remember.

768. I think my neighbor is stalking me as she's been googling my name on her computer. I saw it through my telescope last night.

769. I can totally keep secrets. It's the people I tell them to that can't.

770. Strong people don't put others down. They lift them up and slam them on the ground for maximum damage.

771. Apparently I snore so loudly that it scares everyone in the car I'm driving.

772. Whatever you do always give 100 %. Unless you are donating blood.

773. If you see me smiling it's because I'm thinking of doing something evil or naughty. If you see me laughing it's because I've already done it.

774. I hate when I am about to hug someone really sexy and my face hits the mirror.

775. If I ever need a heart transplant, I'd want my ex's. It's never been used.

776. I'm really good at stuff until people watch me do that stuff.

777. Best friends: Ready to die for each other, but will fight to the death over the last slice of pizza.

778. If I wanted to kill myself I'd climb your ego and jump to your IQ.

779. The difference between "Girlfriend" and "Girl Friend" is that little space in between we call the "Friend Zone".

780. My internet is so slow, it's just faster to drive to the Google headquarters and ask them shit in person.

781. A clean house is the sign of a broken computer.

782. My son asked me what it's like to be married so I told him to leave me alone and when he did I asked him why he was ignoring me.

783. For maximum attention, nothing beats a good mistake.

784. When I told the doctor about my loss of memory, he made me pay in advance.

785. Congratulations, If you press the elevator button three times it goes into hurry mode – really...

786. I like you. You remind me of when I was young and stupid.

787. Any room is a panic room if you've lost your phone in it.

788. People who write "u" instead of "you". What do you do with all the time you save?

789. My husband is on the roof - only a few inches away from an insurance claim that could completely change my life.

790. Top 3 situations that require witnesses: 1) Crimes 2) Accidents 3) Marriages, Need I say more?

791. Never break someone's heart because they have only one inside...break their bones because they have 206 of them.

792. The best things in life are free *plus shipping and handling*

793. I asked my wife what she wanted for Christmas. She told me "Nothing would make her happier than a diamond necklace" So I bought her nothing.

794. Why is there so much blood in my alcohol system?

795. I always tell new hires, don't think of me as your boss, think of me as your friend who can fire you.

796. The last airline I flew charged for everything. Except for the bad service. That was free.

797. My girlfriend told me to go out and get something that makes her look sexy... so I got drunk.

798. Refusing to go to the gym counts as resistance training, right?

799. I bet you $4,567.89 you can't guess how much I owe my bookie.

800. People say money is not the key to happiness, but I always figured if you had enough money, you can have a key made.

801. I remember when Halloween was the scariest night of the year. Now, it's Election night.

802. When I found out that my toaster wasn't waterproof, I was shocked.

803. College is the opposite of kidnapping. They demand $100,000 from you or they'll send your kid back.

804. Masturbation is like procrastination, it's all good and fun until you realize you are only fucking yourself!

805. When I was at school, fifty two percent of the class were good at maths. I was one of the other thirty eight percent.

806. My first child has gone off to college and I feel a great emptiness in my life. Specifically, in my checking account.

807. It must be difficult to post inspirational Tweets when your blood type is B Negative.

808. It's all fun and games until someone loses an eye. Then it's just a game. Find the eye!

809. I love what you've done with your hair. How do you get it to come out of the nostrils like that?

810. Me: Siri, why am I alone? Siri: *opens front facing camera*

811. I'm in a long distance relationship. My girlfriend is in the future.

812. Maybe you need a ladder to climb out of my business?

813. Boy : I have a pen you have a phone number. Think of the possibilities. Girl : I have a sandal you have a face. Think of Casualties.

814. I love my life, but it just wants to be friends...

815. You could very well be going to heaven but it won't be hell in hell without you!

816. Interviewer: "Why do you want this job?" Me: "I've just always been very passionate about not starving to death."

817. You are not as bad as people say, you are much, much worse.

818. Even people who are good for nothing can bring smile on your face, when pushed down the stairs...

819. I typed "married" but it was auto-corrected to "martyred". Damn, smartphone has gained intelligence.

820. Marriage is full of surprises but it's mostly just asking each other "do you have to do that right now?"

821. If you are here - who is running hell?

822. They say you are what you eat, so lay off the nuts.

823. My resolution was to read more so I put the subtitles on my TV.

824. My doctor told me that jogging could add years to my life. He was right—I feel ten years older already.

825. Weddings and funerals are the same because I love going but I don't

want them to be about me.

826. If you don't drink, smoke or do drugs you may live long enough to be a real burden to loved ones. Please pass the wine.

827. How do Asians name their kids? They throw them down the stairs and see what kind of sounds they make

828. My wife made me into millionaire. I was a multi-millionaire before we met.

829. I have one of those unlimited cell phone plans. There's no limit to how much they can charge me.

830. Told my wife I wanted to see our kids every other weekend and she reminded me that we're married and live together so I'd have to see them every day.

831. How come "you're a peach" is a complement but "you're bananas" is an insult? Why are we allowing fruit discrimination to tear society apart?

832. Do you know why I make puns? Because it's my respunsibility.

833. Laughing stock: cattle with a sense of humor.

834. I always put in a full eight hours at work. Spread out over the course of the week.

835. I applied for a job today and they ask for three references. I wrote, "a

dictionary, a Thesaurus, and a map."

836. I don't ignore people, I just choose to not notice them.

837. "Raccoons"? Oh, you mean garbage pandas?

838. I wasn't planning on giving Christmas gifts this year until I heard about those exploding Samsung Galaxy phones.

839. Stephen Hawking says we've got about 1,000 years to find a new place to live. That isn't even enough time for my girlfriend to pack.

840. A clean desk is a sign of a cluttered desk drawer.

841. Sarcasm is just one more service we offer.

842. I recently added squats to my workouts by moving the beer into the bottom shelf of the fridge.

843. 70% of our planet is covered in water, the other 30% is covered in idiots.

844. I am not the kind of girl you can take home to your wife.

845. A wise man once said... Nothing, he only listened.

846. Take an icecube to the bar, smash it and say: "Now that I've broken the ice, will you sleep with me?"

847. I just want to live in a world where people come with on/off switches.

848. People are like trees, if you chop them with an axe they die.

849. I've been running as fast as I can, but I still can't catch my breath.

850. Did you fall from heaven? Cause your face is pretty messed up!

851. The best part about working in an office is that if you ever forget that you got a haircut, someone will definitely point it out to you.

852. You're the best! At being the worst.

853. Before I never used to believe when scientist talk about men evolve from apes... But then I met YOU!

854. If I throw a stick, will you leave?

855. If sex is such a natural phenomenon, how come there are so many books on how to do it?

856. I like the sound of you not talking.

857. You take away the looks, money, intelligence, charm and success and, really, there's no real difference between me and George Clooney.

858. Duck tape fixes everything... Except relationships because she won't let you put it over her mouth.

859. Did something bad happen to you or are you just naturally ugly.

860. My wife still hasn't told me what my New Year's resolutions are.

861. 'Darling, will you catch me if I jump into the water?' 'Darling, if I say yes, will you jump?

862. Marriage advice for dummies:

    Five worst things you can do:

    5. Abandon

    4. Lie

    3. Cheat

    2. Abuse

    1. Forget to start the dishwasher.

863. Men will brag that there are women waiting by the phone at this very moment for their call. Who are these women? Women working at 900 numbers.

864. I'm smiling. This should scare you.

865. I wanted to thank you personally for the like. That's why I'm in your house.

866. I think I married someone else's soulmate. I wish they'd come get him.

867. Men are fun to argue with, because even IF they win... they lose.

868. Have hope for the future, but maybe build a bomb shelter anyway.

869. How to lose an argument with a woman: 1) Argue.

870. I don't worry about terrorism. I was married for two years.

871. Error, no keyboard. Press F1 to continue.

872. It takes two to lie... One to lie and one to listen...

873. Marriage is like a coffin and each kid is another nail.

874. Hi there, I'm a human being! What are you?

875. Ugh, who has time to work out?... I say before a 45 minute nap.

876. I liked beer so much that my family didn't know I drank until they saw me sober!

877. [man] Excuse me, would you like to dance? [women] NO! [man] Maybe u didn't hear me.... I said u look really fat in those pants!

878. Where were you i have been waiting for half an hour. Said No Girl Ever.

879. If I wanted to get trapped in a scary maze, I'd just go into my kid's bedroom.

880. Facebook memories are a great way to see how fat you've gotten.

881. An asteroid 1,200 light years away has a 0.6% chance of colliding with

the Earth, and you all just walking around like everything is fine.

882. You owe me a drink, you're so ugly I dropped mine when I saw you.

883. See no evil, hear no evil, date no evil.

884. Remember a sense of humor does not mean that you tell him jokes, it means you laugh at his.

885. I can't decide which room not to clean first.

886. Never tell a woman that her place is in the kitchen. That's where the knives are kept.

887. Good women are found in every corner of the earth. Unfortunately earth is round.

888. My wife just found out I replaced our bed with a trampoline; she hit the roof.

889. I have the Emergency Alert Warning sound set as the ringtone for when my wife calls.

890. My love for you is like diarrhoea, I just can't hold it in!

891. Please cooperate otherwise it gonna look like rape.

892. Do you want to see a murderer? Kill someone and look yourself in the mirror.

893. You're not fat, you're just... easier to see.

894. I find it ironic that the colors red, white, and blue stand for freedom until they are flashing behind you.

895. Just read that 4,153,237 people got married last year, not to cause any trouble but shouldn't that be an even number?

896. If I had a dollar for every girl that found me unattractive, they would eventually find me attractive.

897. You know you're ugly when it comes to a group picture and they hand you the camera.

898. You know that tingly little feeling you get when you like someone? That's your common sense leaving your body.

899. Isn't it great to live in the 21st century? Where deleting history has become more important than making it.

900. Life is all about perspective. The sinking of the Titanic was a miracle to the lobsters in the ship's kitchen.

901. A recent study has found that women who carry a little extra weight live longer than the men who mention it.

902. When my boss asked me who is the stupid one, me or him? I told him everyone knows he doesn't hire stupid people.

903. Relationships are a lot like algebra. Have you ever looked at your X and wondered Y?

904. That awkward moment when you leave a store without buying anything and all you can think is "act natural, you're innocent".

905. I'm great at multitasking. I can waste time, be unproductive, and procrastinate all at once.

906. Intelligence is like an underwear. It is important that you have it, but not necessary that you show it off.

907. I changed my password to "incorrect". So whenever I forget what it is the computer will say "Your password is incorrect".

908. How do I disable the autocorrect function on my wife?

909. Any married man should forget his mistakes, there's no use in two people remembering the same thing.

910. My wife is so negative. I remembered the car seat, the stroller, AND the diaper bag. Yet all she can talk about is how I forgot the baby.

911. There are two rules for success: 1) Don't tell all you know.

912. Behind every successful student, there is a deactivated Facebook account.

913. It's funny, when I walk into a spider web I demolish his home and

misplace his dinner yet I still feel like the victim.

914. Improve your memory by doing unforgettable things.

915. When an employment application asks who is to be notified in case of emergency, I always write, "A very good doctor".

916. The 50-50-90 rule: Anytime you have a 50-50 chance of getting something right, there's a 90% probability you'll get it wrong.

917. I sometimes watch birds and wonder "If I could fly who would I shit on?"

918. What's worse than waking up at a party and finding a penis drawn on your face? Finding out it was traced.

919. Women spend more time wondering what men are thinking than men spend thinking.

920. My favorite mythical creature? The honest politician.

921. Thanks for explaining the word "many" to me, it means a lot.

922. Dear alcohol, We had a deal where you would make me funnier, smarter, and a better dancer... I saw the video... we need to talk.

923. First word in the world - Huh?

924. I've been repeating the same mistakes in life for so long now, I think

I'll start calling them traditions.

925. My wife had her driver's test the other day. She got 8 out of 10. The other 2 guys jumped clear.

926. I gave up my seat to a blind person in the bus. That is how I lost my job as a bus driver.

927. When I call a family meeting I turn off the house wifi and wait for them all to come running.

928. For me, being "clean and sober" means I'm showered and headed to the pub.

929. She wanted a puppy. But I didn't want a puppy. So we compromised and got a puppy.

930. Funny how they say we need to talk when they really mean you need to listen.

931. Doesn't expecting the unexpected make the unexpected become the expected?

932. Is google a woman? Because it won't let you finish your sentence without coming up with other suggestions.

933. Q: What do you call the security outside of a Samsung Store? A: Guardians of the Galaxy.

934. A good wife always forgives her husband when she's wrong.

935. The light at the end of the tunnel has been turned off due to budget cuts.

936. Wife: "I look fat. Can you give me a compliment?" Husband: "You have perfect eyesight."

937. I asked my wife if she ever fantasizes about me, she said yes - about me taking out the trash, mowing the lawn, and doing the dishes.

938. If time is money are ATM's time machines?

939. Every time you talk to your wife, your mind should remember that... 'This conversation will be recorded for Training and Quality purpose'

940. I can't believe I got fired from the calendar factory. All I did was take a day off.

941. I'm reading a book about anti-gravity. It's impossible to put down.

942. I got caught in police speed trap yesterday. The officer walked up to my car and said "I've been waiting all day for you" Well I said. I got here as fast as I could.

943. Experience is what you get when you didn't get what you wanted.

944. Never get on one knee for a girl who won't get on two for you.

945. TRUE FRIENDSHIP: Walking into a person's house and your wifi connects automatically.

946. Regular naps prevent old age, especially if you take them while driving.

947. There are few things I enjoy more than picking an argument with my girlfriend when she has the hiccups.

948. I'd tell you a chemistry joke but I know I wouldn't get a reaction.

949. I'm the kind of guy who stops the microwave at 1 second just to feel like a bomb defuser.

950. Maybe if we start telling people the brain is an app they will start using it.

951. Cats spend two thirds of their lives sleeping, and the other third making viral videos.

952. Everyone has a friend who laughs funnier than he jokes.

953. The depressing thing about tennis is that no matter how good I get, I'll never be as good as a wall.

954. I need to start paying closer attention to stuff. Found out today my wife and I have separate names for the cat.

955. I'm sorry I wasn't part of your past, can I make it up by being in your future?

956. Dear Couples Who Fight In Public, stop trying to whisper and would it kill you to include some backstory.

957. It looks like your face caught on fire and someone tried to put it out with a hammer.

958. I'm currently boycotting any company that sells items I can't afford.

959. According to most studies, people's number one fear is public speaking. Number two is death. Death is number two. Does that sound right? This means to the average person, if you go to a funeral, you're better off in the casket than doing the eulogy.

960. Sometimes the first step to forgiveness, is realising the other person was born an idiot.

961. eBay is so useless. I tried to look up lighters and all they had was 13,749 matches.

962. I wasn't born with enough middle fingers to let you know how I feel about you.

963. My girlfriends dad asked me what I do. Apparently, "your daughter" wasn't the right answer.

964. The hardness of butter is directly proportional to the softness of the bread.

965. My mom said that if I don't get off my computer and do my

homework she'll slam my head on the keyboard, but I think she's jokinfjreoiwjrtwe4to8rkljreun8f4ny84c8y4t58lym4wthylmhawt4mylt4amlath natyn

966. What do you do if a blonde throws a grenade at you? Pull the pin and throw it back.

967. So apparently RSVP'ing back to a wedding invite 'maybe next time' isn't the correct response.

968. That awkward moment when you're in a meeting and your stomach decides to sound like a dying whale.

969. I'm glad I know sign language, it's pretty handy.

970. Adults are always asking little kids what they want to be when they grow up because they're looking for ideas.

971. The grass is always greener on the other side because its fertilized with bullshit.

972. I like to hold hands at the movies... which always seems to startle strangers.

973. I may not be the brightest nail in the bucket, but at least I have a point.

974. Isn't it weird how when a cop drives by, you feel paranoid instead of protected.

975. The reward for a job well done is more work.

976. If someone hates you for no reason, give that motherfucker a reason.

977. A woman's mind is cleaner than a man's: She changes it more often.

978. A healthy sleep not only makes your life longer, but also shortens the workday.

979. What language are you speaking? Cause it sounds like bullshit.

980. I am known at the gym as the "before picture."

981. Only after getting married you realise that those husband-wife jokes were not just jokes.

982. You are proof that evolution CAN go in reverse.

983. I hate two-faced people. It's so hard to decide which face to slap first.

984. Want to get noticed? Go jogging without moving your arms.

985. What's six inches long, two inches wide, and drives women wild? Money.

986. Thieves had broken into my house and stolen everything except my soap, shower gel, towels and deodorant. Dirty Bastards.

987. What is the difference between men and women? A woman wants one

man to satisfy her every need...A man wants every woman to satisfy his one need.

988. What makes men chase women they have no intention of marrying? The same urge that makes dogs chase cars they have no intention of driving.

989. Roses are red violets are blue, God made me pretty, what happened to you?

990. The reason a dog has so many friends is that he wags his tail instead of his tongue.

991. Wouldn't exercise be more fun if calories screamed while you burned them?

992. Accidentally pooped my pants in the elevator. I'm taking this shit to a whole new level.

993. You haven't experienced awkward until you try to tickle someone who isn't ticklish.

994. You're so fake, Barbie is jealous.

995. Laugh and the world laughs with you. Snore and you sleep alone

996. Makeup tip: You're not in the circus.

997. If you can go to the gym without telling people on the Internet, you

are instantly hired by the CIA.

998. A man enters a store and says: "15 litres of wine please." "Did you bring a container for this?" "You're speaking to it."

999. My speech today will be like a mini-skirt. Long enough to cover the essentials but short enough to hold your attention!

1000. There's nothing like the joy on a kid's face when he first sees the PlayStation box containing the socks I got him for Christmas.

Made in the USA
Columbia, SC
22 June 2020